Field Guide to ™ *Fishing Knots*

Essential Knots for Freshwater and Saltwater Angling

Darren Brown

Illustrated by Mark Woodward

Wilderness
Adventures
Press, Inc.™

Belgrade, Montana

© 2003 Wilderness Adventures Press, Inc.™

Field Guide to Fishing Knots™
Essential Knots for Freshwater and Saltwater Angling

© 2003 (text) Wilderness Adventures Press, Inc.™

Illustrations contained herein © 2003
Wilderness Adventures Press, Inc.™

Published by Wilderness Adventures Press, Inc.™
45 Buckskin Road
Belgrade, MT 59714
Phone: 800-925-3339
Fax: 800-390-7558

Printed in the United States of America

Library of Congress Cataloging-in-Publication Data

Brown, Darren.
   Field guide to fishing knots : essential knots for freshwater and
saltwater angling / by Darren Brown.-- 1st ed.
      p. cm.
  ISBN 1-932098-03-8 (pbk.)
  1. Fishing knots. I. Title.
  SH452.9.K6B76 2003
  799.1'2--dc21

                                        2003010964

Table of Contents

Introduction

Line to Reel

Line to Fly, Lure, Hook, or Swivel

Joining Lines

Fly Line to Leader

Droppers

Boating Knots Every Angler Should Know

Introduction

Most anglers only need to know a few knots in order to fish effectively. But as your angling skills advance (or if you branch out from freshwater to salt or vice versa), you'll find there are specialty knots that work better than other knots in specific situations. There are knots you'll use on every outing and others you'll need only once every year or two.

The knots detailed here are the most common knots used by all types of angler—from bait- or spin-fisher to flyfisher. There are, of course, many more angling knots beyond the ones discussed between these two covers. And if you pursue a highly specialized type of fishing, such as big-game saltwater angling, you will likely benefit from learning a few other unique knots.

For the casual to advanced angler, though, it's probably better to focus on learning to tie a few knots well and then add specialized knots as needed. For instance, a spin-fisher who primarily fishes lures could easily get by with knowing only the Improved Clinch Knot (for attaching lures to line) and the Surgeon's Knot (for joining line to line). For freshwater flyfishers, add a loop knot like the Perfection or Surgeon's Loop and a Nail Knot, and you're more or less set. Serious saltwater anglers will need to know knots like the Bimini Twist, Huffnagle or Albright, Homer Rhode Loop Knot, and several others to cover most situations. And any angler fishing for toothy fish may want to learn the Haywire Twist for attaching wire to the terminal end of the leader.

One of the great things about learning new fishing knots is that you can make it as simple or complicated as you want to. Keeping a quick reference book like this one handy will give you a wide variety of knot options and will refresh your memory on knots you only need once in a blue moon.

Knot-Tying Tips

- Don't be afraid of new knots. Even the most difficult fishing knots can be mastered in just a few minutes. It can be frustrating at first when your fingers don't seem to move like they should or when you feel like you'd need four hands to tie a knot, but with practice you'll be able to tie any knot quickly. Anglers often shy away from knots like the Bimini Twist, but spend a little time learning it and you'll find it's really an easy, fun knot to tie.

- Most fishing line is plain monofilament, but there is also a wide variety of other lines available. It's important to remember that some knots work better than others in specific materials. And even with mono, there will be variations between manufacturers in breaking strength, thickness, stretch, and stiffness. If you are joining line, you'll have the best success with lines of the same brand. Buy quality mono, and experiment until you find the knot that works best for the brand of line you choose.

- Don't store line in direct sunlight, and keep insect repellent and sunscreen away from your line as much as possible. These can all weaken or degrade mono. Also, remember that mono doesn't break down quickly (and fluorocarbon not at all), so don't discard trimmed pieces of line streamside. It's bad for the environment and bad for small animals and fish, which can get tangled in loose line.

- To straighten coiled or kinked mono after storage, pull the line taut and create light friction (warmth) by running your hand up and down the line.

- Much is made of the strength of specific knots, but most knots test at well over 90 percent of line strength (the Homer Rhode Loop Knot being one exception). It's more important to focus on tying the knots you use correctly every time than to worry about which knot is slightly stronger.

- Many failures that are blamed on poor knots are really the result of other factors, like wind knots in your leader or weaknesses caused by abrasion against rocks. Check your line frequently for weak spots. In mono, these often appear as opaque patches and are easy to spot; quickly running your hand up the line will alert you to small nicks or cuts.

- Some knots that cinch down tight against hook eyes can "hinge" after repeated casts, particularly when you're using light line and bigger lures. Check your knot often. Loop knots tend to allow the lure to move more freely, which reduces potential weakness.

- Knot-tying tools are available for many common knots. They usually run from just a few dollars up to around $20. Unless you have failing eyesight, these are rarely necessary.

- For many knots, it's important to follow the instructions precisely for maximum strength. But the stiffness of the material you're using is also a factor. Often, you'll be able to seat a knot better in stiff line with less wraps, while light line can accept additional wraps. Use common sense, and make sure the knot draws down tightly and smoothly.

- Lubricate all knots. Knots seat better when moistened, and the reduced friction during tightening maximizes strength. Most anglers just use saliva, but water also works. Avoid using super-slick products that will prevent the knot from staying put. You'll occasionally read that digestive enzymes from saliva may degrade knots, but it would be tough to find a situation where this is really much of a factor.

- If you need to pull on a hook to tighten a knot, always be sure to pull from the bend of the hook—behind the hook point. Pulling from the hook eye is never a good idea; one slip and you're trying to remove a hook from your hand instead of going fishing.

- There is rarely a need to jerk on line to seat knots. Smooth, even pressure is the best way to draw slack out of knots.

- Once a knot is seated, trim the tag end close to the knot with clippers (biting it with your teeth will leave a longer, ragged end). Never burn the tag end of monofilament as you would some types of rope.

Important Terms

Backing: Thinner line, usually Dacron or occasionally monofilament, used under fly line on a fly reel to fill up the reel and extend the line when playing large fish.

Double Line: Created with knots like the Bimini Twist or Spider Hitch, double lines are often used by record-seeking anglers to strengthen a section of leader.

Leader: Line that connects lure, hook, or fly to the rest of the line (or fly line). The "butt" end of a tapered leader is the heavy, stiff section that attaches to fly line.

Shock Tippet: A section of thicker leader material or wire that protects against abrasion caused by toothy fish or rocks.

Standing Line: The main part of the line, usually going to the body of the line or to the reel.

Tag End: The end of the line, where the knot is tied, or the very tip of the line.

Tippet: Line at the terminal end of the leader (next to the fly, hook, or lure) or forming sections of the leader near its end.

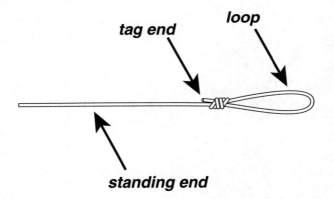

Line to Reel
Arbor Knot

The Arbor Knot is a very simple knot designed to secure monofilament or backing to the arbor of any type of reel. Any knot that slides down to tighten without a lot of bulk would work well for this job (such as the Uni Knot), but it would be difficult to find an easier knot than this one.

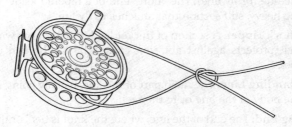

1. Loop the tag end of the line over the spool and tie an overhand knot around the standing line.

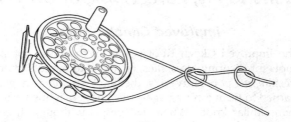

2. Tie a second overhand knot above the first.

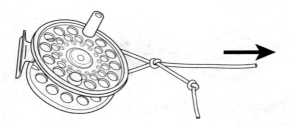

3. Lubricate and tighten by pulling on the standing line until the two overhand knots slip together snugly against the reel arbor. Trim the tag end.

Line to Fly, Lure, Hook, or Swivel

Improved Clinch Knot

The Improved Clinch Knot is one of the most popular knots for securing lures, flies, or hooks to monofilament. Despite its popularity—it's the knot so many anglers learned to tie at a young age—this knot is slightly weaker than similar knots. When tied properly, though, it is a perfectly serviceable knot for most applications. The Improved Clinch Knot is best for lighter line, as it becomes difficult to tie in stiffer material.

1. Thread the tag end through the hook eye.

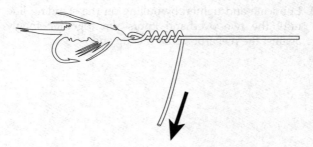

2. Twist it 3 to 6 times around the standing line.

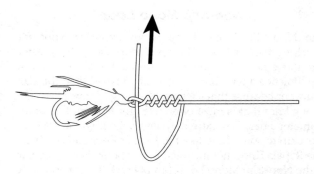

3. Push the tag end through the loop formed at the hook eye.

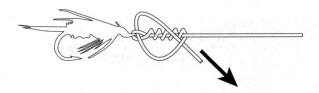

4. Bring the tag end through the loop formed between the hook eye and the top of the knot.

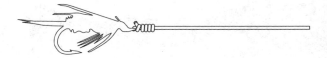

5. Lubricate and tighten by pulling on the standing line and hook. (Keep your fingertips behind the point of the hook.) The coils should sit down smoothly and evenly against the hook eye.

Non-Slip Mono Loop

The Non-Slip Mono Loop is an excellent knot for attaching flies or lures. The open loop allows for greater lure movement. As the name implies, the loop does not slip. Practice a few times to get the finished loop the size you want because that's where it's going to stay. It's a very strong knot that is most often used for light and medium diameter lines. For extremely heavy line, you'll need to move up to something like the Homer Rhode Loop Knot. The Rapala Knot (not included in this book) is very similar to the Non-Slip Mono Loop. Simply tuck the tag end back through the last loop before tightening and you've tied the Rapala.

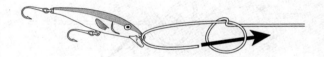

1. Make an overhand knot in the tag end (but don't tighten) before inserting the end through the hook eye.

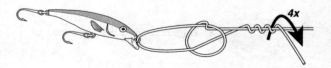

2. Bring the tag end back through the overhand loop (make sure it enters from the same side it exited) and wrap it several times around the standing line.

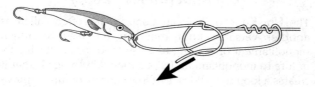

3. Bring the tag back through the overhand knot (again making sure it enters from the same side it exited).

4. Lubricate and tighten by pulling on the bend of the hook with one hand and the standing line with the other, making small adjustments to control the size of the final loop. Trim tag.

Uni Knot (Duncan Loop)

The Uni Knot, or Duncan Loop, as it's often called, is another versatile knot that can be used to attach monofilament or backing to a reel arbor or to attach a fly or lure to monofilament. Its one main advantage is that it creates a loop that slides. To allow your fly or lure to move more freely, simply open the loop. It will generally stay open under the light pressure of casting and then close tightly when a fish is hooked. Once the fish has been landed, the loop can be opened again without untying the knot. Steelhead and salmon anglers probably use this application more than most other anglers.

The Uni Knot can be incorporated into a variety of other knots, so it's a good one to know.

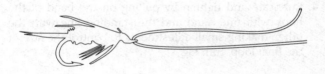

1. Pass the tag end through the hook eye.

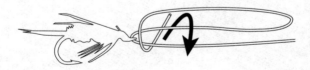

2. Create a long narrow loop in the tag end (above the standing line).

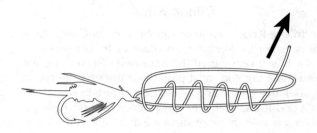

3. Wrap the tag end 4 or 5 times around the standing line and one side of the loop and bring the tag through the loop on the final pass.

4. Lubricate and tighten by pulling on the tag and standing ends. (When making a small loop in front of a fly or lure, adjust it to the right size and then hold the loop while pulling gently on the tag end with forceps.)

Trilene Knot

The Trilene Knot is another variation of the Clinch Knot that is useful for joining monofilament to flies, lures, or hooks. It is stronger than the Improved Clinch Knot, but because the tag end must pass twice through the eye of the hook this knot can only be used in certain situations. You'll find it impossible to thread line twice through the eye on a smaller hook or to create and tighten the loops with stiffer monofilament. Use this knot primarily with larger hooks and lighter line (12-pound test and down, which is roughly 2X for flyfishers).

1. Insert the tag end through the hook eye and bring it around and back through again, creating two small loops in front of the hook eye.

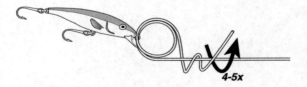

2. Hold the loops in place while wrapping the tag end around the standing line 5 or 6 times.

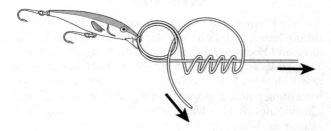

3. Bring the tag back through the small loops.

4. Lubricate and tighten. Trim tag.

Orvis Knot

The Orvis Knot is a relative newcomer in the world of fishing knots, and it's an excellent choice for joining flies, lures, and hooks to monofilament. Most anglers learn just a few knots and stick with them for life, but this is another worth learning, particularly if you are looking for something a little stronger than the ubiquitous Improved Clinch Knot. It also forms a small, clean-looking knot against the hook eye.

Much like the Uni Knot, it can be used to create a small sliding loop next to the hook, allowing the fly or lure to move more freely in the water. It will tighten smoothly under pressure and can be opened again without weakening the knot. The Orvis Knot is also a good choice when attaching larger lures or flies to light line because loop knots put less stress on the line around the joint.

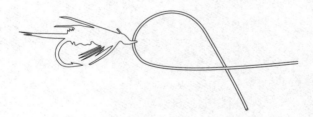

1. Bring the tag end through the hook eye from the bottom and form a small loop in front of the eye.

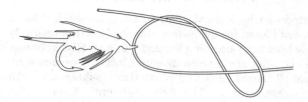

2. Make a second loop by bringing the tag around the standing line and back through the first loop.

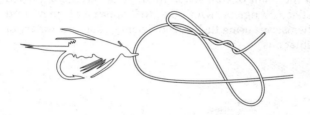

3. Bring the tag back through the second loop and make two turns around the far side of the loop.

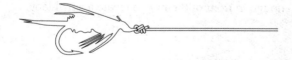

4. Lubricate and tighten the second loop against the standing line. Finish tightening by pulling on the lure and standing line to cinch the knot against the hook eye. Trim tag end.

Sixteen-Twenty Loop Knot

Introduced by Richard Nightingale in his book *Atlantic Salmon Chronicles*, the Sixteen-Twenty Loop is a relatively new knot for connecting line to fly or lure. (The knot was named after the Sixteen-Twenty Club, whose members have all caught 20-pound-plus Atlantic salmon on a #16 or smaller hook.) The Sixteen-Twenty Knot works particularly well in lines testing 12 pounds or less, and it creates a small, strong knot. Like many loop knots, it's useful when you need to attach delicate tippets to large hooks. The tightened loop allows a little more movement at the point of connection than knots like the Improved Clinch. Anglers who like to experiment may find themselves using the Sixteen-Twenty Loop in a variety of situations.

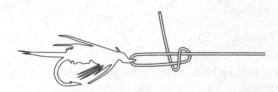

1. Insert the tag end through the hook eye and bring it far enough in front of the lure to create a small loop.

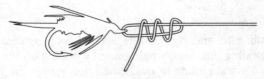

2. Wrap the tag end around the loop several times, moving toward the lure.

3. Hold the wraps loosely in place and bring the tag back through the top wrap.

4. Lubricate and tighten by pulling on the tag end to close the wraps around the leader. Then pull hard on the standing line to draw the knot up against the hook eye. The knot's creator notes that you should hear a small pop or click when the knot seats properly.

Palomar Knot

The Palomar Knot is one of the easiest fishing knots to tie, and it's very strong. Its main disadvantage is that the line must be doubled before it is threaded through the hook eye, so it can't be used with smaller hooks. Also, the loop must pass over the fly or lure, which can be a hassle with bulkier flies or large lures with multiple hooks. Still, for a large bare hook or a swivel, it's a great knot—and easy on nighttime anglers or anglers with failing eyesight.

1. Double the tag end and pass it through the hook eye.

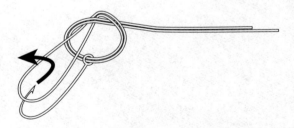

2. Make an overhand knot with the doubled line (around the standing line), leaving a loop in the end.

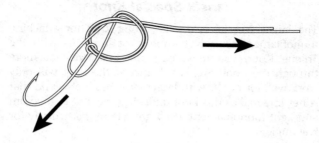

3. Bring the hook through the loop and pull on the standing and tag ends to begin tightening.

4. Lubricate and finish tightening by pulling on the standing end. Trim tag.

Jansik Special Knot

The Jansik Special is a very strong knot for attaching monofilament to swivels, hooks, or lures. As with the Trilene Knot, you must pass the line twice or more through the hook eye, which means the knot will only work well for hooks with larger eyes. You'll also find that stiffer line makes this knot difficult to tie. But in medium and light monofilament, it's a great knot, particularly for bait anglers.

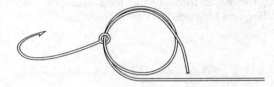

1. Insert the tag end up through the hook eye, bring it around in a small loop, and insert it through the eye again.

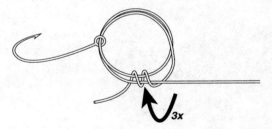

2. Bring the tag under the standing line and wrap it several times around the standing line and loops you've created.

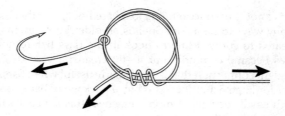

3. Lubricate and pull on the bend of the hook and the standing and tag ends of the line to tighten. (You may need to hold the tag between your teeth to do this.)

4. Tighten securely and trim tag.

Snelling a Hook

This knot is used to join line to a bare hook, and there are many ways to tie it. The Snell is an older knot, originally created to connect line to hook in the days before hook eyes became common, but it still creates a very strong, straight connection that is particularly useful when fishing bait for large fish. When you buy a package of bare hooks with small sections of mono attached, this is usually the knot you'll find connecting hook to line.

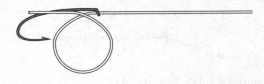

1. Insert line through the eye and form a loop next to the shank.

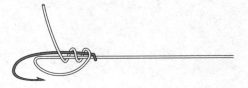

2. Begin wrapping the tag around the shank and the bottom of the loop (much like a Uni Knot), working toward the bend of the hook.

3. After 5 or 6 wraps, lubricate and pull on the tag end to begin tightening.

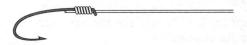

4. Seat the knot tightly by pulling on hook and standing line, using forceps or pliers if necessary. Trim tag.

Crawford Knot

The Crawford Knot doesn't seem to be as popular as a lot of other knots, but it works perfectly fine for attaching hooks, lures, flies, or swivels.

1. Insert the line through the hook eye and form a loop with the standing line.

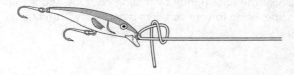

2. Bring the tag end under the standing line and back over the whole loop.

3. Form a figure-8 around the outside of the loop.

4. Bring the tag through the front of the loop.

5. Tuck the tag end back through the bottom of the loop (next to the hook eye). Lubricate, tighten, and trim tag.

Berkley Braid Knot

The Berkley Braid Knot was designed specifically for attaching lures, hooks, and flies to the new Super Braid lines. There are a variety of other knots, or variations of knots, that work well with these new lines, but this one is solid and easy to tie.

1. Double the tag end of the line and pass it through the hook eye.

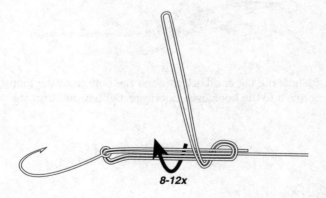

8-12x

2. With the doubled line parallel to the standing line, bring the tag end over the doubled line and standing line and wrap back toward the hook.

3. Make 8 to 10 wraps.

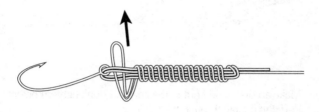

4. Insert the tag end through the small loop just in front of the hook eye.

5. Lubricate and tighten by pulling on the tag and standing ends. Trim tags.

Homer Rhode Loop Knot

The Homer Rhode Loop Knot is really only useful for attaching lures or flies to very heavy line. It's a weak knot (only around 50 percent strength), but that shouldn't matter in large diameter lines. It's a good alternative to the Non-Slip Mono Loop only in the stiffest of materials.

1. Make an overhand knot in the line (but don't tighten) before inserting the tag through the hook eye.

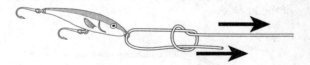

2. Bring the tag back through the overhand knot (make sure it enters from the same side it exited).

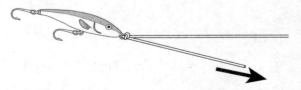

3. Tighten the overhand knot, sliding it down against the hook eye.

4. Make another overhand knot around the standing line and adjust it to the size you want the finished loop to be (keep the loop small).

5. Tighten the second overhand knot (forceps or pliers will help, as this knot will be tied in heavy line).

6. Pull on the standing line and the first overhand knot should slide back against the second, creating the finished loop. Trim tag.

Offshore Swivel Knot

The Offshore Swivel Knot is a versatile and simple knot that was originally designed for attaching swivels for big-game saltwater angling. It also works well for attaching hooks to a section of double line (with a Bimini Twist or Spider Hitch). It's particularly noted for its strength, as the knot usually holds even if one strand breaks.

1. Insert the doubled line through the swivel eye and twist it once.

2. Keeping the twist in the line, bring the end of the loop back to the standing line. You should now have two loops.

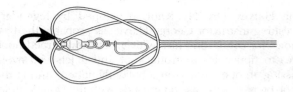

3. Hold the loops open and pass the swivel through them 6 times or so.

4. Release the end of the loop and begin tightening by pulling on the standing double line.

5. Lubricate and tighten completely, using forceps or pliers to seat the knot in stiffer line.

Harvey Dry Fly Knot

The Harvey Dry Fly Knot, developed by legendary flyfishing instructor George Harvey, is probably the best choice for connecting flies with up or downturned hook eyes to tippet. It's a strong knot and it lets you avoid passing an open loop over a bulky fly pattern during the knot-tying process, as you must do with the Double Turle.

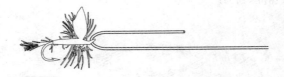

1. Insert the tag end through the hook eye and bring it back toward the standing line.

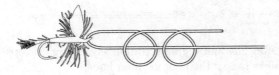

2. While holding the standing and tag ends just in front of the fly, make a small loop around the standing line, then make another of the same size and hold the two loops together.

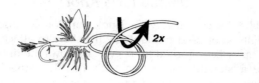

3. Push the tag end through the loops and make two wraps around them.

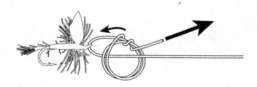

4. Hold the bend of the hook in one hand and pull on the standing line with the other to cinch the knot. If you've done it right, the two loops will slide back and pop over the hook eye, leaving a straight connection between line and fly. Trim tag.

Double Turle Knot

Just like the Harvey Dry Fly Knot, the Double Turle is a specialty knot used primarily by flyfishers to attach flies with up or downturned hook eyes. It allows the tippet to make a straight connection with the fly, rather than coming off at an awkward angle. If you find it difficult to pull larger flies through the loop this knot requires, switch to the Harvey.

1. Insert the tag end through the hook eye and form a loop with a double overhand knot in it.

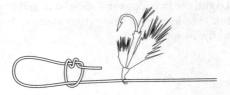

2. Hold the loop while tightening the double overhand knot. (You can also "improve" the knot by pushing the tag end of the double overhand knot back through the loop before tightening.)

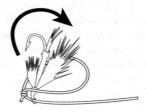

3. Open the loop wide enough to fit over the fly and pass the fly through the loop.

4. Pull on the standing line until the knot slides down against the hook eye. Trim tag.

Riffling Hitch

The Riffle or Riffling Hitch (also called the Portland Creek Hitch) is basically just a Double Turle Knot with one or two Half Hitches added behind the head of the fly to make it ride higher in the water. Flyfishers chasing steelhead and salmon sometimes use this knot to "skitter" a fly across the surface of the water.

1. Start by tying a Double Turle Knot.

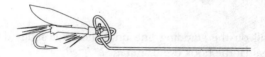

2. Make two Half Hitches over the head of the fly behind the hook eye.

3. Pull tight.

Haywire Twist

The Haywire Twist is a specialty knot that works best in single-strand wire. Wire is useful as part of the leader when you are fishing for toothy saltwater gamefish or freshwater species like northern pike and muskie, which usually aren't too leader shy.

One common approach is to put a Haywire Twist in each end of a short piece of wire—one through the hook eye of the fly or lure and the other connecting to the rest of the leader with a loop-to-loop connection or directly to a swivel.

1. Insert the tag end of the wire through the hook eye (either close against the eye or leaving a small loop to allow the lure to move more easily) then twist it around the standing line 4 or 5 times.

2. Move the tag end perpendicular to the standing end and wrap it several times around the main line (tightly).

3. To trim the tag end of the wire, gently bend it back and forth until it breaks off. Make sure the tag sits tightly against the final wraps. (Don't cut the wire, as that will leave a sharp edge.)

Figure-8 Knot

The Figure-8 Knot should only be used for connecting wire—particularly braided wire—to flies, lures, or hooks. While it's not strong enough for monofilament connections, it does make a solid connection in braided wire. If you are using single-strand wire, though, the Haywire Twist might be a better choice.

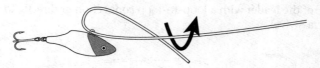

1. Insert the wire through the hook eye and bring it back around the standing line.

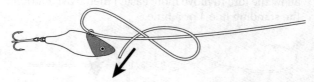

2. Loop the tag end of the wire around the standing line again and insert it through the first loop you created.

3. You should be able to see the figure-8 as you draw the knot tight.

4. Trim the tag end.

Joining Lines

Surgeon's Knot

The Surgeon's Knot is a strong, versatile knot used to join sections of leader, particularly those of unequal diameter. It is faster and easier to tie than the Blood Knot, which also works well for many line-to-line connections. Once you try this simple knot, you won't soon go back to trying to hold everything in place while threading the tag ends through the center of those laborious Blood Knots.

1. Overlap the lines to be joined.

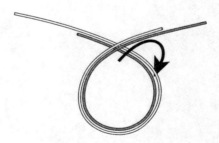

2. Form a simple loop.

3. Tie a double or triple overhand knot by passing the tag end of the larger diameter line and the standing end of the lighter line through the loop two or three times. (Make sure that the tag end goes through the loop with the longer standing line each time.)

4. Lubricate and tighten by pulling on all four ends. Trim the two tag ends.

Blood Knot

The Blood Knot is great for joining lines of similar diameter. It makes a slightly smoother connection than the Surgeon's Knot, but it takes longer to tie and is a little more difficult to tie well. And for maximum strength, it's important to tie this knot perfectly.

If the lines vary in diameter a little more than .002 inch, you're better off switching to the Surgeon's Knot. If the variation is a great deal larger, it might be wise to use a loop-to-loop connection or try an Albright Knot. If you'd rather stick with the Blood Knot, you can also try doubling the lighter of the two lines before starting to tie the knot. This is a tough knot to tie in very stiff line.

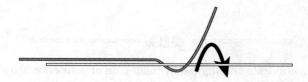

1. Overlap the lines to be joined, leaving yourself plenty of line to work with. Cross the lines at the point where you want to make the knot and hold this area securely as you begin to wrap one of the tag ends around the standing line.

2. Take 4 or 5 turns around the standing line and then bring the tag end back through the "fork" you created where the lines cross.

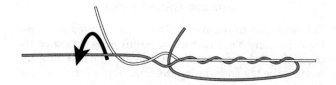

3. Hold everything securely while you wrap the other tag end around the standing line 4 or 5 times. (Making one less wrap in the stiffer of the two lines often helps seat the knot better.)

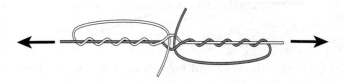

4. Pass the second tag end through the loop that now forms at the center. Make sure it passes through in the opposite direction from the first tag end.

5. Lubricate and tighten by pulling on the standing ends while holding the tag ends in place or pull on all four ends at once. (This is tricky at first without a couple of extra hands, but you'll get the hang of it. Some anglers hold the tag ends between their teeth while they pull on the standing ends.) Trim the tag ends.

Simple Blood Knot

This variation of the Blood Knot (first detailed in a knot book by Lefty Kreh and Mark Sosin) is as strong as the original and easier to tie. If you struggle with inserting and holding the tag ends during the final steps of the standard Blood Knot, this knot will make your life a lot easier.

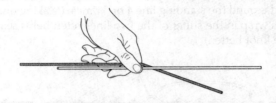

1. Overlap the lines and hold them at the point where they will be crossed.

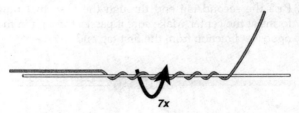

2. Wrap the right tag end 7 times around the standing line.

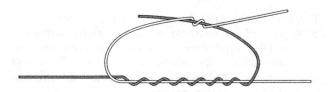

3. Wrap the left tag end around the right tag 7 times, holding the previous wraps in place.

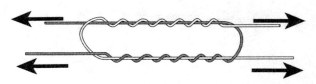

4. Lubricate and tighten by pulling on the tag ends and then the standing lines. Alternate until the knot draws down smoothly and tightly.

5. If tied correctly, the tag ends you trim should be on opposite sides of the knot.

Loop to Loop

This isn't really a knot, but loops like the Perfection Loop or Surgeon's Loop (see next two knots) can be interlocked to join lines of different diameter—or even different materials—with quick reliable connections. There isn't much to joining the two loops, but to achieve full strength it is important that they are seated properly.

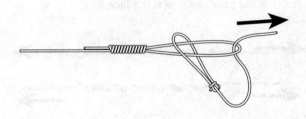

Pass one loop over the other and pull the rest of the leader through the second loop.

Correct

Incorrect

Perfection Loop

The Perfection Loop creates a loop with a small, clean knot that stays perfectly in line with the leader. While many casual anglers stick with the Surgeon's Loop, there are situations where a Perfection Loop might be preferable—such as when you are making a delicate presentation to leader-shy trout in a crystal-clear spring creek or when using heavy, stiff leader material where the alignment of the leader will be more noticeable.

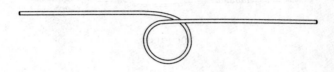

1. Form a loop near the end of the line, with the tag end crossing under the standing line.

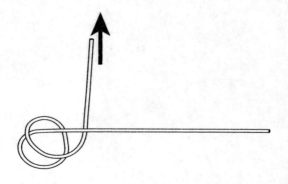

2. While holding the first loop in place, make a second loop on top of the first and pass the tag end under the standing line.

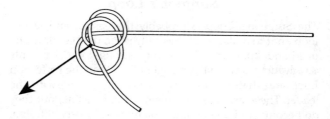

3. Bring the tag end back between the two loops, and then pull the second loop through the first.

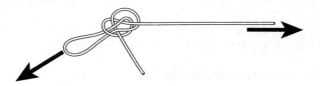

4. Lubricate and tighten by pulling on the loop and the standing line.

5. Trim tag.

Surgeon's Loop

The Surgeon's Loop is probably the easiest and fastest loop knot to make, as it's basically just a double (or triple) overhand knot. It's also a very strong loop. The only disadvantages are that it is a bit bulkier than the Perfection Loop and that it doesn't stay smoothly in line with the leader. These are rarely problems in lighter line, but they do become an issue in larger diameters. In very stiff line, this knot doesn't work very well at all, as it's difficult to tighten.

You can also use this knot as an alternative to the Non-Slip Mono Loop for attaching flies or lures. Simply thread the line through the hook eye before doubling the line.

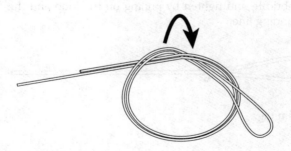

1. Double the end of the line.

2. Make an overhand knot.

3. Pass the doubled end of line through the loop of the overhand knot two or three times.

4. Lubricate and tighten by pulling on the end of the loop with one hand and the tag and standing line with the other. (You can manipulate the size of the final loop by making slight adjustments before tightening.) Trim tag.

Spider Hitch

The Spider Hitch is a loop knot primarily used in saltwater angling. It creates a good strong loop that can be used for a variety of loop connections or to create double-line sections in a saltwater leader. It's often used as an easier-to-tie substitute for the Bimini Twist.

1. Double a section of line and then form a small reverse loop.

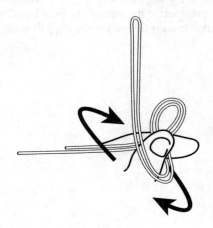

2. Hold the loop between thumb and index finger and then wrap the doubled line around the thumb and small loop 6 or 7 times.

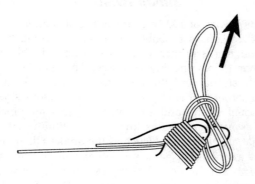

3. Push the doubled tag end through the loop.

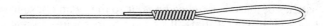

4. Lubricate and tighten by pulling on the loop and the tag and standing lines. Trim tag end.

Bimini Twist

The Bimini Twist, or 100 Percent Knot, as it is often called for good reason, is probably the ultimate fishing knot, even though it is primarily used to create a double line rather than to join one line to another. This double line is incredibly strong, and the knot itself acts as a kind of shock absorber that is able to handle tremendous stress. Most casual fresh- and saltwater anglers—and many experts as well—avoid this knot by substituting strong knots that are easier to tie (such as the Spider Hitch). But if you are a serious big-game saltwater angler or if you are going for an IGFA class-tippet record, it's an indispensable knot to have in your arsenal.

Despite the fact that it is included in a "field guide," this is certainly not a knot you should attempt for the first time while on the water. Even experts usually tie up batches of these before heading out so they won't have to fool with it while fishing. It's a knot that requires a great deal of line to tie—5 or 6 feet—but don't let that intimidate you. It's a fun knot to tie, and not at all difficult once you get the hang of it. The Huffnagle Knot (or Albright Knot) is usually the best choice for connecting separate line to a Bimini Twist.

1. Double a section of line. Hold it together with your left hand and put your right forefinger through the end of the loop. Rotate your hand to put 20 to 40 twists in the line.

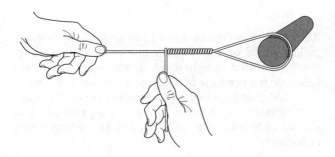

2. Secure the loop around a stationary object (your knee works well), keeping the twists intact. Pull the tag and standing ends apart to tighten the twists against each other. With the tag end held tightly at a right angle to the standing line (which should be aligned straight with the loop), pull gently on the standing line with your left hand while using your right hand to coax the tag end to "jump" or roll over the first twist by keeping it taut and moving it away from your body.

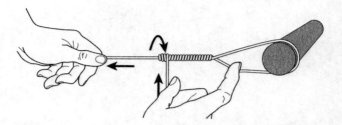

3. Once you have the new row of twists started, continue pulling gently on the standing line while adding line to the twists with your right hand. Do this by pressing down lightly on the near side of the loop with your right forefinger while giving the twists line from the tag end. (It takes a little practice to get this right, but making sure you have smooth tight coils right up to the fork in the loop is very important.)

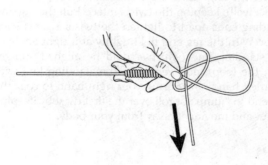

4. Keep tension on with both hands while working your left hand up toward the coils. Once you are holding the wraps firmly in your left hand, put a Half Hitch around one side of the loop.

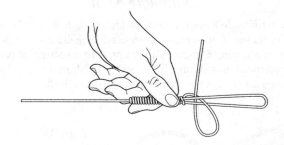

5. Make another Half Hitch around the other side of the loop. After one or both of these Half Hitches, it should be safe to release the tension you've been holding in the knot.

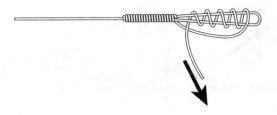

6. Make a small loop in the tag end and wrap several times back toward the main knot, making sure to go around both sides of the big loop.

7. Lubricate and tighten completely. If tied correctly, all the wraps will sit neatly next to each other.

Huffnagle Knot

The Huffnagle Knot is useful for joining light line to heavy monofilament. It is most often used by saltwater anglers to join a larger diameter shock tippet to a section of class tippet that has a Bimini Twist tied in it (shown here). This creates a very strong connection without a bulky knot.

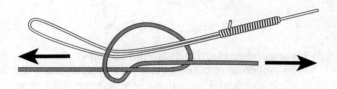

1. Make an overhand knot in the heavier leader and insert the loop of the Bimini Twist through the center.

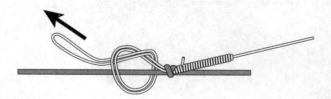

2. Tighten the overhand knot against the base of the Bimini and trim the tag, then tie an overhand knot in the Bimini (around the standing line).

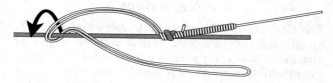

3. Tighten the second overhand knot against the first, then make a loop with the tag end of the doubled line of the Bimini.

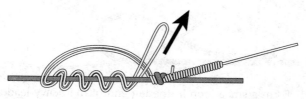

4. Wrap the tag end several times back through the loop (toward the main knot).

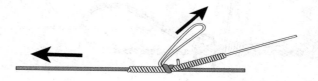

5. Lubricate and tighten against the main knot.

6. Secure the knot by pulling on the tag end of the Bimini with one hand and the standing leader with the other. Trim tag end.

Albright Knot

The Albright's usefulness lies in its ability to join lines of greatly different diameter and/or different types of material. It works very well for joining braided or single-strand wire to monofilament and is most often used in saltwater applications. It is also a handy knot for joining backing to fly line, although many anglers use a Nail Knot for this.

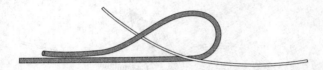

1. Form a small loop in the tag end of the heavy leader and insert the end of the lighter line through the loop.

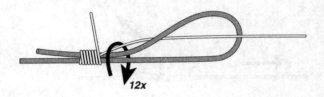

2. Wrap the tag end of the lighter line around itself and the doubled heavier line about a dozen times, working back toward the loop.

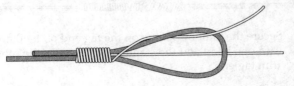

3. Bring the tag end back through the loop.

4. Bring the knot tight by pulling on the standing end of the light line (hold the wraps in place as they are cinched down). Pull on the standing and tag ends to secure completely.

5. Make a small loop in the tag end of the light line and start wrapping back toward the main knot.

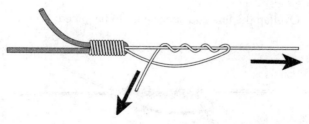

6. Lubricate and seat this small Clinch Knot by pulling on the tag and standing ends of the light line.

7. Trim tag ends.

Double Uni Knot

While its lack of strength makes the Uni Knot less useful than comparable knots in many situations, tying this knot back to back as a Double Uni Knot makes a solid leader-to-leader connection, particularly when using specialized material like "shock gum." This stretchy material acts as a shock absorber within the leader when fishing for large fish with very light line.

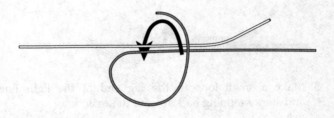

1. Overlap the line and shock gum to be joined.

2. Make a Uni Knot with one tag end.

3. Tighten this knot and make sure there is enough line to repeat the process with the other tag.

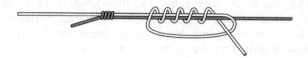

4. Tie another Uni Knot in the other tag end.

5. Tighten the second knot and slide the two knots back to back, making sure everything is snug and tight.

6. Trim tag ends.

Fly Line to Leader

Nail Knot

The Nail Knot, often called the Tube Knot, is the most popular knot for joining fly line to leader and fly line to backing in fly angling. It's a smooth, attractive knot and actually gets stronger as more pressure is applied to it. Some anglers coat this knot with waterproof, flexible cement to ensure that it doesn't catch on the rod guides, but this is rarely necessary.

Few people tie the Nail Knot with an actual nail these days, but it can still be done that way. It's not difficult to tie, but it takes a little practice to tie it with the heavy butt sections that come with most leaders. (In very stiff material, it helps to use less wraps.) With practice, you'll be able to keep the coils tight and in line as you seat the knot. It's very easy to see if a wrap has "jumped" out of line as the knot is drawn tight.

This also isn't a knot you'll need to tie all that often because when your leader wears down you can simply cut it back to around 6 to 12 inches and tie a Perfection Loop or Surgeon's Loop in the tag end. When you add a new leader, just tie another loop in the butt section to make a quick loop-to-loop attachment. This works fine until it is time to replace your entire fly line.

There are several variations of this knot that have proved useful in specific situations.

Tube Nail Knot

This standard version of the Nail Knot utilizes a narrow tube—a small straw works well. The tube replaces the nail, which was originally used to stiffen the area being wrapped. With the tube, passing the tag end back through the coils is much easier.

1. Hold a small tube parallel to the end of the fly line and extend the butt of the leader about a foot beyond this area.

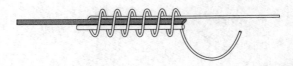

2. Wrap the butt section 6 or more times around the tube and fly line (tightly), moving back toward the end of the fly line. Hold the coils firmly in line.

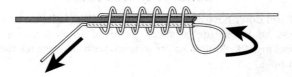

3. Via the tube, pass the end of the leader back through the coils.

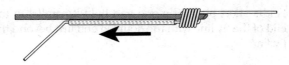

4. Carefully hold everything in place as you pull on both ends of the leader—not the fly line—and withdraw the tube. (Again, make sure the coils don't jump out of line.)

5. The knot should cinch down neatly. Pull everything tight and trim the tag ends.

Mono Loop Nail Knot

If you don't have a small tube handy, this variation allows you to substitute a short piece of monofilament or backing. (Backing is easier to work with because it's more supple.)

1. Fold a short piece of mono and hold it parallel to the end of the fly line with the doubled end just beyond the fly line.

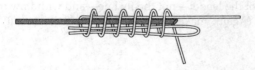

2. Wrap the butt section of leader 5 or 6 times toward the end of the fly line, keeping the coils slightly loose (but holding them firmly in line with thumb and forefinger).

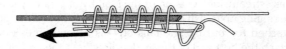

3. Insert the tag end of the leader through the doubled end of the mono and carefully pull the short piece of mono out through the coils you are holding in place. The mono will bring the tag end of the leader through the coils (away from the end of the fly line).

4. Discard the short piece of mono, and tighten the knot by pulling on the tag and standing ends of the leader—not the fly line—while making sure the coils stay in line.

5. Trim tag ends.

Fast Nail Knot

This "streamside" version of the Nail Knot is handy if you are rigging up to fish and the braided loop that comes pre-attached to your fly line falls off—as it sometimes does. Attach the butt end of the leader directly to the end of the fly line with this knot, and you'll be ready to fish in just a minute or two.

This knot is easier to tie if you just cut off a short piece of the butt section instead of using the entire leader. When you're finished, tie a Perfection Loop or Surgeon's Loop in the tag end and join it to the leader with another loop. You can use anything from a toothpick (shown here) to a paper clip, needle, nail, etc. to stiff the base while making the wraps.

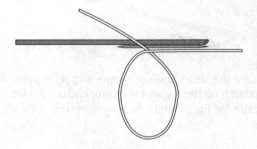

1. Hold the toothpick parallel to the end of the fly line. Next, form a loop in the butt section of leader, with the tag toward the standing fly line.

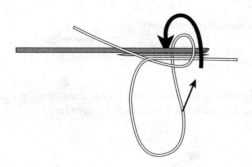

2. Hold the loop, toothpick, and fly line in place and begin wrapping the right side of the loop from right to left. (It may be difficult to get started while holding the coils, but you'll get it.)

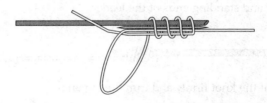

3. Wrap the line around the leader, toothpick, and fly line 5 or 6 times, while keeping a firm hold on the coils. (You'll see why it helps to just use a short piece of the leader butt, as you have to clear it out of the way on each wrap.)

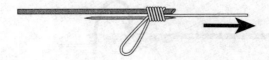

4. Hold everything in place and pull on the standing end of the leader until the knot starts to tighten.

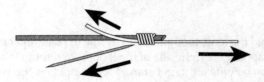

5. Slide the toothpick out and continue to tighten the knot (while keeping the coils in line) by pulling on the tag and standing ends of the leader.

6. Seat the knot firmly and trim the tag ends.

Double Nail Knot

The Double Nail Knot is useful for joining together very stiff leader material or for joining Super Braid line.

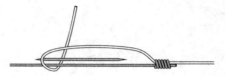

1. Tie a Nail Knot with one tag end, leaving plenty of room in the tag end of the other line. Tighten the knot, but don't secure it completely.

2. Tie another nail knot behind the first one.

3. Adjust the knots so they are back to back and finish tightening. Trim tag ends.

Nail-less Nail Knot

The Nail-less Nail Knot is particularly useful for attaching backing to fly line, as backing material is usually more supple than the stiff butt sections of leader material (making it easier to manipulate the wraps or coils).

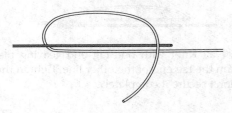

1. Overlap the end of the fly line with the end of the backing. Form a loop in the backing.

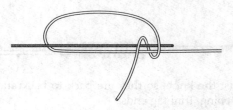

2. Wrap the tag end of the backing around the fly line, going through the loop on each pass. Hold these wraps in place as you go.

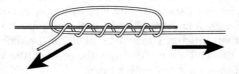

3. Pull on the tag and standing ends of the backing to seat the knot.

4. Finish tightening and trim the tag ends.

Needle Knot

The Needle Knot is very similar to the Nail Knot, but it creates an even smoother fly line-to-leader connection. It's definitely a knot you'll want to tie at home, however, rather than attempt streamside, as it can be difficult to thread the stiff mono through the eye of the needle without shaving it first with a razor.

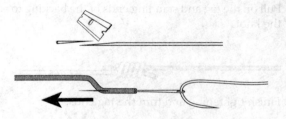

1. Thread the butt section of the leader through the eye of a needle—the smaller the better. (Shaving the end of the leader to a point makes this much easier.) Next, push the needle through the end of the fly line and bring it out the side about 1/4 inch from the end.

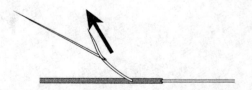

2. Remove the needle (but keep it handy) and pull a little more of the leader through the hole you've created.

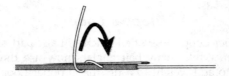

3. Lay the needle beside the fly line with the eye extending just beyond the end.

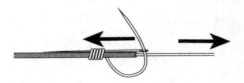

4. Wrap the tag end of the leader 5 or 6 times (from left to right) toward the end of the fly line. Make the wraps fairly tight, but not too tight, and then thread the tag back through the eye of the needle.

5. Pull the needle through the coils, remove it from the tag end that was pulled through behind it, and tighten the knot by pulling on the tag and standing ends of the leader—not the fly line. Trim the tag end.

Droppers

Dropper Loop

A Dropper Loop can be tied quickly in any part of a line or leader. While many bait anglers now use three-way swivels to add weight to a rig, the Dropper Loop is still handy for quickly adding an extra sinker or hook where it's needed along the line. Fly anglers also use it occasionally.

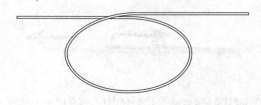

1. Make a small loop in the line.

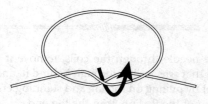

2. Wrap one side of the loop around the standing line 3 to 6 times. (This should create an even number of twists on both sides of the line you are wrapping.)

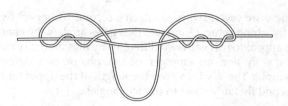

3. Reach through the loop in the center of the wraps and pull the bigger loop back through.

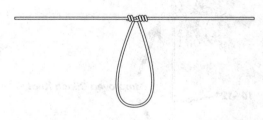

4. Lubricate and tighten by pulling on both standing lines.

Two-Fly Rigs

There are several ways to attach a second "dropper" fly to a flyfishing setup. Using two flies gives anglers the chance to appeal to fish with two different dry flies on the surface, a dry fly and an emerger or nymph, or two different nymphs. The key is to keep the length of the tippet for the second fly fairly short to reduce tangles.

Hook Eye

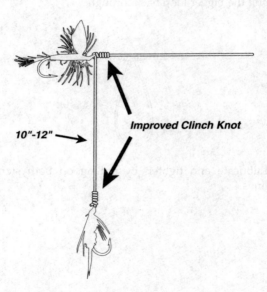

10"-12" →

Improved Clinch Knot

This method works well if you are using a big dry fly with a large hook eye as the lead fly. Smaller hook eyes don't allow enough room for two knots. This method also seems to have a greater effect on how the lead fly floats, as a trailing nymph pattern can draw it down at the eye.

Bend of the Hook

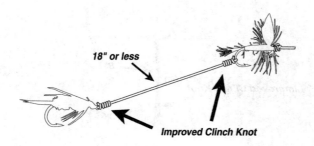

18" or less

Improved Clinch Knot

Attaching a second fly to the bend of the hook on the first fly is probably the most popular method for fishing a two-fly rig. It's relatively easy to add a quick Improved Clinch Knot in that location and the flies seem to tangle less often. Remember to keep the tippet between flies around 18 inches or less. If you are fishing two nymphs and you need to add weight to get them closer to the streambed, add split shot between the two flies instead of in front of the lead fly.

Blood Knot

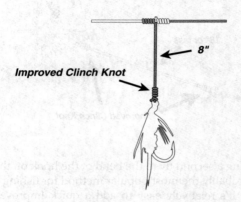

8"

Improved Clinch Knot

This method isn't used too often these days because it's harder to tie and tangles more often, but it's still a viable option. Simply leave the tag end of the heavier line in your Blood Knot about 8 inches long and attach a fly directly to it. If you attach the second fly to the tag end of the lighter tippet, you'll have to deal with more tangles.

Boating Knots Every Angler Should Know

These rope knots aren't technically fishing knots, but they are knots every angler will probably use at some point, particularly when fishing from a boat.

Bowline

The Bowline is an excellent all-around rope knot for making a non-slip loop. It is quick to tie, doesn't slip, and can be easily untied no matter how tight the knot. If you fish from a boat, you'll undoubtedly need this knot at some point.

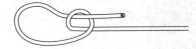

1. Form a small loop in the standing line—the farther back from the end you make this loop, the bigger the finished loop—and bring the tag end of the rope up through it.

2. Bring the tag end around the standing line and back through the small loop.

3. Tighten. (To undo this knot, press on the "bight," which is located next to the standing line.)

Half Hitches

While the Bowline is a better knot for securing a boat, knowing how to throw a couple of quick Half Hitches into a rope will come in handy for a variety of connections. Wrapping the rope twice around the stationary object will help prevent the Half Hitches from slipping. Keep in mind that this is more of a "tension" knot, meaning it won't hold as well if waves are hitting the boat and continually pushing slack and then tension into the line.

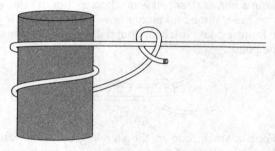

1. Wrap the rope twice around the stationary object, then bring the tag end over the standing line and back through the gap just created.

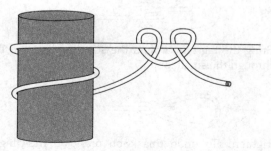

2. Repeat in front of the first Half Hitch and tighten.

Trucker's Hitch

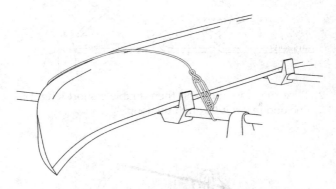

The Trucker's Hitch is a useful knot for tying canoes and small boats to roof racks, truck beds, or trailers. The webbing and buckles of the newer tension straps have reduced the need for this knot, but you'll be glad you know it if you need to secure a boat with just rope. The knot allows you to keep tension on the rope while tying off.

1. Secure one end of the rope to the rack with a bowline, throw the rope over to the other side of the boat, then make a small loop in the tag end, leaving plenty of line to finish the knot.

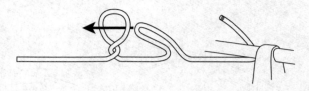

2. Twist the loop once and then double a short length of line and insert it through the loop.

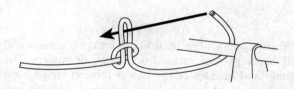

3. Tighten this loop, then bring the tag end around the rack and back up through the loop you just created.

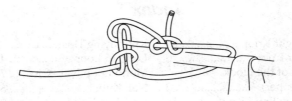

4. Pull the tag end back toward the rack and cinch it down. This creates the tension that secures the boat to the rack. When you have it as tight as you want it, throw two Half Hitches into the line.

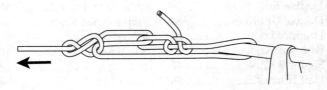

5. Tighten the Half Hitches down against the small loop.

Index

FIELD GUIDE SERIES
AND
FLY FISHING GUIDE SERIES

If you would like to order additional copies of this book or our
other Wilderness Adventures Press guidebooks, please fill out
the order form below or call
1-800-925-3339 or *fax 800-390-7558.* Visit our website for a
listing of over 2000 sporting books — the largest online:
www.wildadv.com   *Mail To:*

Wilderness Adventures Press, Inc.,
45 Buckskin Road • Belgrade, MT 59714

☐ **Please send me your quarterly catalog on hunting and
fishing books.**

Ship to:
Name _____

Address _____

City _____
State_____ Zip_____

Home Phone_____
Work Phone_____

Payment: ☐ Check   ☐ Visa   ☐ Mastercard   ☐ Discover
☐ America Express

Card Number _____
Expiration Date_____

Signature _____

Qty.	Title of Book	Price	Total
	Field Guide to Dog First Aid	$15.00	
	Field Guide to Upland Birds and Waterfowl	$19.95	
	Field Guide to Fishing Knots	$14.95	

Qty.	Title of Book	Price	Total
	Flyfisher's Guide to Chesapeake Bay	$28.95	
	Flyfisher's Guide to Colorado	$28.95	
	Flyfisher's Guide to Freshwater Florida	$28.95	
	Flyfisher's Guide to the Florida Keys	$28.95	
	Flyfisher's Guide to Idaho	$28.95	
	Flyfisher's Guide to Montana	$26.95	
	Flyfisher's Guide to Michigan	$26.95	
	Flyfisher's Guide to Minnesota	$28.95	
	Flyfisher's Guide to New York	$28.95	
	Flyfisher's Guide to Northern California	$26.95	
	Flyfisher's Guide to Northern New England	$28.95	
	Flyfisher's Guide to Oregon	$28.95	
	Flyfisher's Guide to Pennsylvania	$28.95	
	Flyfisher's Guide to Texas	$28.95	
	Flyfisher's Guide to Utah	$28.95	
	Flyfisher's Guide to the Virginias	$28.95	
	Flyfisher's Guide to Washington	$28.95	
	Flyfisher's Guide to Wisconsin	$28.95	
	Flyfisher's Guide to Wyoming	$28.95	
	On the Fly Guide to the Northwest	$26.95	
	Saltwater Angler's Guide to the Southeast	$26.95	
	Saltwater Angler's Guide to Southern California	$26.95	
Total Order + shipping & handling			

**Shipping and handling: $4.99 for first book,
$3.00 per additional book, up to $13.99 maximum**